The abacus contest : stories
from Taiwan and China
Author: Wu, Priscilla.
Reading Level: 4.7 MG
Point Value: 1.0
ACCELERATED READER QUIZ# 44294

P9-DIJ-217

The Abacus Contest

The Abacus Contest

Stories from Taiwan and China

Priscilla Wu

◆

Illustrated by Xiao-jun Li

fulcrum kids
Golden, Colorado

For Ishiung, Jessica and Paloma,
with much love and affection

Copyright © 1996 Priscilla Wu

Cover and interior illustrations copyright © 1996 Xiao-jun Li

All rights reserved. No part of this publication may be reproduced, stored in a retrieval system or transmitted in any form or by any means, electronic, mechanical, photocopying, recording or otherwise, without the prior written permission of the publisher.

Library of Congress Cataloging-in-Publication Data

Wu, Priscilla
    The abacus contest : stories from Taiwan and China / Priscilla Wu ; illustrated by Xiao-jun Li.
        p. cm.
    Summary: In a small city in southern Taiwan, six children with a traditional background experience different changes in their outlook.
    ISBN 1-55591-243-5
    [1. Taiwan—Fiction.]   I. Li, Hsiao-chün, ill.   II. Title.
PZ7.W9623Ab   1996
[Fic]—dc20   95-41552
                                                                              CIP
                                                                              AC

Printed in the United States of America

0 9 8 7 6 5 4 3 2 1

Fulcrum Publishing
350 Indiana Street, Suite 350
Golden, Colorado 80401-5093
(800) 992-2908

Table of Contents

Introduction

✦

The stories in this collection take place during the present in the small manufacturing city of Chiai in southern Taiwan. They are the result of several visits to my husband's home and family over a fifteen-year period. Although the stories are set in one town, they could have happened in many small cities in both Taiwan and China.

In terms of language, culture and religion, Taiwan is in many ways a miniature China. Aboriginal tribes inhabited Taiwan during prehistoric times. Wars and invasions on mainland China prompted successive waves of immigrant migrations into Taiwan. One of the first immigrant groups was the Ke Jia Ren. Their Chinese dialect is Ke Ren and they trace their roots back to the cradle of Chinese civilization, the Yellow River Valley.

Approximately eighty percent of the immigrants who settled Taiwan came from the southern Chinese province of Fukien. They speak the Chinese dialect of Fukien Min Nan. The most recent wave of immigrants came to Taiwan from mainland China in 1949 with Chiang Kai-shek. These people came from all over China, and many of them spoke Mandarin as well as their local dialects.

The different Chinese dialects denote slightly different customs, such as a special type of cake or flower arrangement at a wedding ceremony. But the majority of the Chinese population has the same religious practices and customs. In Taiwan and China, almost identical arts, crafts, cuisine and cultural expressions thrive.

The children in these stories are like children everywhere. Their customs and cultural values, however, are in some ways dissimilar from those of children in the United States. In "Saying Good-bye to Ah Ma," the funeral rites are different from most funeral rituals in the United States. There is much emphasis in Chinese families for children to do well in school. This cultural value runs through "The Abacus Contest" and "Ping Mei's Wish." "Returning to the Ancestral Home" affirms the important place that ancestors, elders and the family unit have in Chinese society. The fact that religion and spirits play an important part in the day-to-day life of people in Taiwan is evident in "Zong Zong Goes to Disneyland." "Bright Eyes," a story about competition and attachment, could have happened in many locales, except that pigeon racing and other cultural details unmistakably set it in today's Chinese world.

The
Abacus Contest

Stories from Taiwan and China

◆

The Abacus Contest

◆

Gao Mai's fingers flew back and forth over the smooth black beads of the abacus.

Suddenly a wire snapped. The beads bounced onto the desk and rolled across the floor.

Gao Mai fell to her knees and crawled around after them. Just as she reached for the last bead, her best friend Li Zhi kicked it away from her hand. The other children giggled. Gao Mai's face burned.

Gao Mai opened her eyes wide and sat up in alarm. What an awful dream!

The comforting aroma of steamy, overcooked rice drifted in from the next room. She pushed aside the heavy quilt, got up from the floor and put on her school uniform.

"Are you ready for the big day?" Gao Mai's mother asked her as she came into the main room of the apartment. Gao Mai sat down at the table and helped herself to dried meat, eel and pickled cucumber.

The dream was fresh in her mind. "I'm not sure," she said.

"Remember what I told you," said Gao Mai's father. "Imagine the abacus is part of you." He smiled at her. "You did so well when we practiced."

It was true. During a few of her many timed drills she was even faster than her father. And he used the abacus every day at the bank.

"Don't worry," said her mother. "You're one of the best abacus students in your class."

"But what about Li Zhi?" asked Gao Mai. "She's beaten me every year."

"Last time it was only by one second. You've improved so much, I'm sure you'll win. Besides," continued her mother, as she lit the incense on the altar where the family ancestors were honored, "you were born under the lucky sign of the horse. I went to the temple yesterday and said a special prayer for you."

Gao Mai looked at her watch. "I have to go."

"Good luck," said her mother.

"Good luck," said her father. "I'll be thinking about you all morning."

Gao Mai ran downstairs to the street and walked quickly through the open market. One farmer had spread a piece of burlap on the pavement and piled it high with cut sugarcane. Her mouth watered as she thought of sucking the sweet juice from the snowy white center. Gao Mai glanced at the fish swimming around in a shallow metal pan. Tonight they would be on someone's plate, maybe even her own.

She reached the school just as the bell rang. Outside her classroom some boys were playing jian zhi. Her classmate, Kun Pei, scored one point after another by kicking the jian zhi into the air over and over again without letting it hit the ground.

Gao Mai walked into the classroom and Kun Pei yelled: "I won!"

During last year's abacus contest Li Zhi had beaten Kun Pei by four seconds, and Gao Mai had beaten him by three seconds. Today she was hoping to beat both of them.

Gao Mai watched Li Zhi's braids bounce as she tapped everyone on the way to her desk. She knew Li Zhi loved practical jokes and could tell by her mischievous look that she might play one at any moment. Gao Mai smiled while thinking of jokes they had played on their classmates together. Last week they had even played one on Li Zhi's mother. Yesterday Li Zhi had invited her to come over after school today so that they could think of a trick to play on her brother, Da Wei.

"Don't forget who won last year," said Li Zhi, sitting down behind her. She tugged on Gao Mai's ponytail and giggled.

"That was last year." Gao Mai leaned away and said, "If you pull my hair again, I'm not going to your house today."

Li Zhi leaned forward to grab Gao Mai's ponytail but only caught the tip. Gao Mai started to say: That's it, I'm not going to your house today. But the teacher arrived and the class stood up to greet him.

"Ni hao?" said Mr. Wang. "While everyone is nice and fresh, we'll begin with the abacus contest." He passed out booklets filled with addition, subtraction, multiplication and division problems.

"Open to the first page and begin with number one. When all the exercises are completed, return your booklet to my desk and I'll write the final time. Ready?" He paused. "Begin!"

Gao Mai's left hand moved down the column of numbers rapidly, wrote the answers and turned the test pages. The fingers on her right hand flew back and forth among the smooth, black beads of the abacus.

In a few minutes she was writing the last answer to the addition problems. Gao Mai began subtracting and a moment later heard pages turning. Everyone was right behind her!

She worked carefully. It was easy to make a subtraction mistake, especially when exchanging a higher bead for lesser ones.

After finishing the last subtraction problem she heard Li Zhi's page turn.

Gao Mai frantically turned to the multiplication but two pages were stuck together. She pulled them apart with shaking hands.

Barely breathing, Gao Mai sped through the multiplication and division. Finally she wrote down the last answer, jumped from her seat and collided with Li Zhi.

Two desks in front of them, Kun Pei rushed up and dropped his booklet on the teacher's desk.

"Oh, no!" yelled Li Zhi. "It's not fair!" She and Gao Mai dropped their booklets on the desk immediately after him.

"Quiet down, everyone," said the teacher.

Gao Mai returned to her desk and slumped in the seat, unaware of the other students handing in their booklets. Her bad dream had come true.

"Time for recess," said Mr. Wang, "while I check the answers."

Gao Mai was the last to go outside.

"Come on," yelled Ping Mei, wanting her to come and jump rope. But she shook her head. Across the playground, Li Zhi motioned for her to come and play tag with some of their friends. But Gao Mai turned away.

As he kicked the jian zhi into the air, Kun Pei bragged to a group of boys about winning the abacus contest. Gao Mai thought of her father's jian zhi at home on top of the TV. Father! Gao Mai knew he'd be disappointed that she hadn't won. The bell rang and everyone piled back into the classroom.

She heard Li Zhi behind her, laughing. "Hurry up, slowpoke!" she said, pushing past her.

Gao Mai secretly wished she could be carefree, like Li Zhi.

Mr. Wang stood up with the winning certificates in his hand. "Third-place winner of this year's abacus contest is Zong Zong."

The class applauded and a small girl with thick glasses walked quickly to the front of the room and shook hands with the teacher.

"The second-place certificate goes to Kun Pei," Mr. Wang continued.

Kun Pei came forward, looking as if he were about to cry.

"You were first to get your booklet in," Mr. Wang said as he handed him a certificate. "But one answer was wrong."

Gao Mai was confused. She turned around and looked into Li Zhi's bewildered face.

"Now," began the teacher, "we have an unusual situation—one that has never happened to me before. First place in speed and accuracy goes to Li Zhi, last year's first-place winner, and also to Gao Mai, last year's second-place winner.

Gao Mai turned and looked at Li Zhi. They burst out laughing and hurried to the front of the room.

"Here's a first-place certificate for both of you," said Mr. Wang.

As Gao Mai shook hands with the teacher, she decided it was a good day to go to Li Zhi's, after all.

Bright Eyes

◆

Kun Pei tossed his backpack on the couch and ran upstairs to the roof of his building. The cooing grew louder as he approached the large, wooden cage. He opened the chicken wire door and glanced around until he saw a soft brown pigeon with pale pink tail feathers. Picking it up with both hands, he stroked the large, powerful flight muscles.

"Are you ready for tomorrow?" he whispered.

The pigeon cooed softly.

Kun Pei examined the tag on Bright Eyes' leg to make sure his name and phone number were legible. He remembered the day he had purchased Bright Eyes. Kun Pei had thought he would never be able to afford a pigeon from such expensive stock. But his father had encouraged him to save his New Year's money, and then his favorite uncle had presented him with the difference. He was determined to show both of them that he had made a good investment and that Bright Eyes was indeed a champion.

Kun Pei heard steps on the stairs and turned to see his father coming toward him.

"Let them all out," said his father. "They should be exercised before tomorrow."

The pigeons were released from the large cage. Kun Pei saw Bright Eyes take off and then watched the rest of the group intently. "There's Rainbow Throat," he said, pointing to a slate gray pigeon with a ripple of color on its neck and chest. "I wish we could race more than two pigeons."

"I do, too," said his father. "If we win this race, we can afford to enter Speckles next time."

"By that time her chicks will be hatched," said Kun Pei.

"Then she'll really fly home quickly."

"But what if something happens to her?"

"The chicks will be old enough to hand feed," replied his father, "and I know you can help with that."

Kun Pei watched the pigeons circling high above the building. He tried to pick out Bright Eyes.

"There she is," Kun Pei's raised finger slowly moved through the air. "I can see her white chest."

"Time to eat!" They turned and saw Guai Li, Kun Pei's younger sister. "Ma Ma says to hurry up and wash your hands."

"Okay," said Kun Pei's father, "we'll be down in a minute." He glanced up and saw some pigeons heading for the cage. "Oh no! Where's the flag?"

Kun Pei handed his father a broomstick with a large, red flag attached to it. His father waved it vigorously. The pigeons flew over the cage instead of landing on it.

"That's Lazy Wings and her friends," said Kun Pei. "She always comes in early."

"She and Bright Eyes are so different."

"I know," said Kun Pei.

"I bet it has to do with all that special training and handling you've given her."

"Maybe," said Kun Pei, proudly. He didn't want to brag, but it was true. Bright Eyes was their fastest pigeon and tomorrow would be her first big race. He couldn't wait, because he knew she was a champion.

Kun Pei woke before his alarm clock sounded. He dressed quickly in the early morning light and went into the kitchen. His mother and father were already there. He went over to the rice cooker and ladled out some chi fan. Then he sat down at the table and helped himself to salty eggs and pickled vegetables.

"There's a storm coming in from the south," said his father.

Kun Pei lowered his chopsticks. "Is it a big one?"

"It's hard to tell. I won't know until I get down to the coast." He paused. "I was thinking maybe we should race Speckles instead of Bright Eyes. The older pigeons are more reliable in bad weather. "

"Bright Eyes can do it. I know she can," said Kun Pei.

"Well," said his father, "this is her first big race and I wouldn't want to lose her in bad weather."

"I *know* she can do it," said Kun Pei. "Remember how well she did when you took her to Taitung in the rain?"

"That's true."

"Why don't you take all three and then decide which ones to race when you get down there?" asked Kun Pei's mother.

"That's a good idea," said his father.

Kun Pei agreed, but it was a terrible disappointment. For weeks and weeks he'd planned for this race. He'd even picked out the handheld video game that he was going to buy with his share of the winnings. The rest of the winnings would be used for entrance fees in next month's race.

"Well," said his father, standing up, "unless it's very bad weather, I'll race Bright Eyes."

Kun Pei ran upstairs to the cage with three pigeon cases. Moving quickly, he spotted Speckles and Rainbow Throat and put them each into a case. Then he picked up Bright Eyes.

"Remember," he said softly, holding the pigeon close, "come back as quickly and safely as you can."

He would wait all morning for her return. There would be many obstacles on her hundred-kilometer flight. Besides bad weather, there was even a pigeon thief ring. Birds were known to be kidnapped when they stopped to eat on long flights. Then they were ransomed to the owner. The thought made Kun Pei shiver. "And stay away from the pigeon thief ring," he said sternly to her through the wire mesh on her case.

Holding one case under his arm and the other two by the handles, Kun Pei carefully negotiated the stairs and went out to the car where his mother and father were waiting.

"I should be down at the coast by ten," said his father. "The race starts at eleven, so the pigeons, if all goes well, should be home by one." He looked over at Kun Pei. "Give the signal as soon as you see them, so they'll come in immediately. Then go quickly to Mr. Chen's and register the time." He looked at his wife. "When Kun Pei leaves, go up to the roof and watch for the other pigeon, in case it comes in while he's at Mr. Chen's."

They put the pigeons in the car and Kun Pei's father got in. "I should be home by three, at the latest," he said. He put the car into gear, smiled at each of them and drove off.

Kun Pei looked up at the sky as he walked across the street to his front door. The clouds to the south were thick and dark. He went up to the roof to wait.

Around lunchtime his mother brought him a plate with two chicken bao zhi dumplings.

"Why don't you come inside for a while?" she asked. "It looks like it's about to rain."

"I can't." He picked up the bao zhi with his chopsticks and bit into the snowy surface.

In a little while Kun Pei felt a soft sprinkle of spring rain. His mother reappeared. "Come on in," she said.

"No," he answered. "They'll be here soon."

His mother went downstairs and brought back a yellow slicker that he pulled over his head while looking up at the sky.

"There's one!" he yelled, running over and opening the cage door. Kun Pei and his mother watched the sky intently.

"It's Rainbow Throat," said his mother.

The pigeon landed on the edge of the cage and Kun Pei quickly put it in the case. Then he ran downstairs and out the door.

A few moments later Mr. Chen was logging Rainbow Throat's time.

"It looks like you've come in second," said Mr. Chen. "Mr. Shu's brown and white one was here about five minutes ago."

Kun Pei jumped up and down. That would mean enough prize money for his video game, as well as entrance fees for the next race. He ran home as fast as he could, trying hard not to shake Rainbow Throat's case.

"We won! We won!" he yelled to his mother after returning to the roof. "Rainbow Throat came in second." He carefully took the pigeon from the case and set it next to the food and water. Rainbow Throat sucked water for a long time while Kun Pei re-filled the food bowl.

"It should be easy to see Bright Eyes now that the weather's clearing," said his mother, glancing back and forth across the sky.

"What time is it?" asked Kun Pei.

She looked at her watch. "Almost two o'clock. I'm going down to wait for your father. He should be home soon."

Kun Pei stared at the sky for the next hour, until he heard his father on the staircase.

"We won!" shouted his father, coming toward him.

Kun Pei went straight to the pigeon case in his father's hand.

"Speckles," he said quietly, wishing more than anything it was Bright Eyes.

"The weather wasn't bad when I arrived, so I released Bright Eyes. Isn't she back yet?"

"No," said Kun Pei. "She's so fast. Why isn't she home?"

"Don't worry," said his father. "Maybe she flew off course. I'm going to have some lunch. Why don't you come inside for a while?"

"I will in a few minutes," he said.

But he stayed there until Guai Li came upstairs.

"Time for dinner!" she said. "Ma Ma says you have to come."

He stood up and started down the steps slowly. If only Bright Eyes were home by now.

The next morning, Kun Pei dressed quickly for school and ran up to the roof. In a moment he was back downstairs in the kitchen.

"Still no sign of Bright Eyes?" asked his mother.

Kun Pei hung his head and didn't answer.

"Remember when we were training Gray Wings and she didn't come back for a long time?" asked his father.

"But it wasn't this long," said Kun Pei, picking at his chi fan. "I'm not hungry." He got up and put on his backpack. "Bye," he said.

"But you haven't eaten anything," said his mother.

"I'll be okay," he said, going out the door.

On the way to school he browsed among the street vendors' merchandise. Next to a rack of clothing was a table with school supplies and a variety of handheld video games. Automatically, he reached for one. Then he drew back. It reminded him of how much he'd wanted Bright Eyes to win. Now it seemed so unimportant. He only wanted her to return safely.

He thought about the time someone's cat had gotten into the pigeon cage. There was blood everywhere and three pigeons had been killed. He'd rushed over, afraid that Bright Eyes was one of them. But there she was, perched on the clothesline safe and sound. He'd felt sorry for the other pigeons, but the thought of losing Bright Eyes was much worse.

All day at school he moped around. Mr. Wang even asked him if he was sick.

"I'm okay," he lied.

On the playground his friends could hardly believe that he'd forgotten to bring his jian zhi to school.

He arrived home and dropped his backpack on the kitchen floor.

"Take that fresh water up to the pigeons," said his mother, motioning toward a bucket next to the stairs.

The thought of going to the cage and not seeing Bright Eyes was too much to bear. "I can't," he said. "I'm too tired."

"Do what your mother asks," said his father.

Kun Pei picked up the metal handle and slowly carried the sloshing water upstairs.

Suddenly he ran back downstairs shouting. "She's back! Bright Eyes is back!"

His parents came to the bottom of the staircase.

"I got a call this morning from a man in Kaohsiung who was exercising his pigeons when the race was going on," said his father. "Evidently Bright Eyes got sidetracked and followed his pigeons home instead of coming back here. He just realized this morning that she was in his cage. That's when he called and I drove down and picked her up."

"Whew!" said Kun Pei, collapsing onto a kitchen chair. "I thought we'd never see her again."

"She may be fast," said his father, "but I'm not sure how good her homing instincts are."

"I don't care," said Kun Pei. "All I want is for her to be safe and sound." He rushed back upstairs to change the water and give Bright Eyes an extra helping of grain.

Saying Good-bye to Ah Ma

◆

The crying seemed endless. Day after day the relatives paid their respects to the long, red casket lying in the entrance to the family's old hotel. Da Wei, Li Zhi's older brother, had sobbed inconsolably for the first few days of the seven-day funeral ceremony. Now he was tired of all the services and wanted to play with his friends. But his mother had told him it was disrespectful to be so carefree before his grandmother was buried.

Once, when he was five years old, he had danced around the street with chains of fake money around his waist. Suddenly, in the midst of all his fun, his mother had grabbed him, pulled off the chains and dragged him home. It was a long time before he understood the money was a religious offering and his mother had acted so harshly because she feared retribution from the gods.

Every day from dawn to dusk, the monks, nuns and a Buddhist priest—resplendent in bright orange—performed one service after another in front of the hotel. Sometimes his mother let him do his homework or go off with his friends, but there were certain services, like this one, that she insisted he attend.

Da Wei watched the ritual. The priest offered the multicolored cords to his parents, aunts and uncles. They pulled each cord, undoing the knot above the tassel. Now his Ah Ma was released from all earthly ties and her spirit could migrate to heaven.

If they passed the knotted cord to him, although he knew they wouldn't, he would never pull it free. He would keep her here, in this world, even if she were only a spirit. His eyes welled with tears. Angrily, he brushed them away.

It was better to be at school. Then he could forget what was happening. But here, with the constant chanting and incense and his Ah Ma's picture on the makeshift altar, it was impossible.

He looked over at Li Zhi. She had cried the first couple of days but now was herself again. If only he could let go of his Ah Ma so easily!

He remembered when Ah Ma had played hide-and-seek with him. He'd hide from her underneath the staircase while she called and called his name. But Ah Ma never found him. Finally he'd hear her voice. "Da Wei! I give up. Come out, come out, wherever you are!" He swallowed hard. Never again would he hear her call his name.

The next morning he woke to the sound of drums, cymbals and chanting outside his window.

"Put these on," said his mother, handing him the dark mourning garments.

He pulled the loop around the last brocade button and picked up the straw headdress lined with yellow cloth. Looking in the mirror, he straightened it and then went downstairs. For a moment he stopped and stared at the picture of his grandfather, Ah Ma's husband, on the family altar. He had died when Da Wei was three, ten years ago. Da Wei barely remembered the funeral.

The outside altar was now rearranged to form seven steps, one for each level of heaven.

All morning Da Wei sat perspiring in the hot tropical sun while friends and local dignitaries praised his grandmother. Half listening, he thought about how little these people really knew his Ah Ma. How could they? Did they have breakfast with her every morning? Did she bring them soups and herbal drinks when they were sick and fevered? They could never miss her like he would.

The service concluded and he watched his parents and relatives kneel and pour whiskey into a bowl and onto the dirt. Thus his Ah Ma's spirit was commended to the gods of heaven and earth.

The coffin was fitted with a wooden brace and a group of barefoot, ragged men slowly carried it out into the street. Once outside, two marching bands broke into "Auld Lang Syne" and five elderly men struck up dissonant chords on folk instruments.

As he watched the coffin leave the hotel, Da Wei was overwhelmed with nausea. He ran inside to the bathroom and threw up in the toilet. Soon they would be taking the coffin to the cemetery. His Ah Ma had lived in this house with him his whole life. There was never a day she had not been there for him. He was her favorite.

He heard his name. They were calling him for the procession that would march through town on the way to the cemetery. Again and again he heard his name. But he couldn't move. The bathroom door opened. It was Li Zhi.

She turned quickly and ran, shouting, "Ma, Ma! I found him! Ma, Ma! I found him! He's hiding in the bathroom."

His mother appeared. "Are you all right? It's time to go. Everyone is waiting."

"I'm not going."

"Don't shame me!" She grabbed him by the arm and pulled. But he didn't move.

"I'm not going," he repeated.

"Come right now or I'll call your father."

Da Wei covered his face and sobbed.

His mother burst into tears and pulled him toward her. "I'm sorry," she said, hugging him. She gently wiped his face with a wet handkerchief. "I miss her, too," she said, biting her lip. "It will be so hard without her." She choked back sobs. "But we have each other." She pulled him close again. "Here," she said, handing him a dry handkerchief.

He wiped his eyes and blew his nose.

"Okay?" she asked, stroking his head.

He nodded and they went to join the others.

The priest, nuns and monks headed the procession through the city. Da Wei lined up behind the casket with the rest of his family. Then came the long line of flower trucks, bands and mourners wearing different colored headdresses, depending on their relation to Da Wei's grandmother.

The walk through main thoroughfares and narrow side streets was exhausting in the noon heat. Da Wei struggled to keep up. His mandarin jacket stuck to his back. Finally the band broke into "Auld Lang Syne" again and Da Wei saw the buses, lined up across the street, that would take everyone to the cemetery.

The crowded bus sped, honking, through the narrow streets and finally reached the outskirts of the city. A cool breeze and pleasant country sights and smells rushed in to refresh Da Wei. Often the bus balked on the steep mountain slope, but then recovered to continue its climb. Rested and revived by the ride, Da Wei stepped off the bus with the other mourners when they reached the cemetery.

The surrounding monuments were dwarfed by towering vegetation. Gentle rays of afternoon sun penetrated the green ceiling. Soothing, cool mountain breezes rippled the leaves. Such a peaceful place!

The hired crew removed the casket from the truck. Before it was lowered into the open grave, Da Wei's mother came over to him. "We were both born the year of the cow," she said. "It's bad luck for us to see her buried."

They went down the hill and joined a few other people who were also waiting a short distance from the burial site.

"Maybe it's easier not to see her lowered into the ground," said his mother.

Da Wei wasn't sure. But he felt peaceful thinking of his grandmother in this beautiful place. They went back up the hill and his mother joined his father's family as they circled the fresh burial site. Then one of the monks gave each of them a handful of grain, coins and nails. They sprinkled the grain on the grave site.

"What are these for?" asked Da Wei, as his mother handed him the coins and the nails.

"The grain is for the earth, the coins are for prosperity and the nails are so that you will have many sons."

Before getting on the bus, Da Wei picked one of the wild orchids growing in the lush undergrowth.

During the ride home, Da Wei turned his face into the cool breeze and thought of the spirit world. Where was she now? Somewhere between here and there. Would she migrate to the highest level of heaven? He felt so.

The bus stopped in front of the hotel. It looked bare without the funeral trappings of the last seven days. Da Wei followed his family over to the fire blazing on the edge of the street. One by one they took off their rice weave headdresses and threw them into the fire.

Da Wei watched the flames leap and fall and the strawlike strands darken and curl. Then the fire died down. It reminded him of his own sadness and anger. First it had consumed him and then it slowly diminished and finally subsided.

His father took his Ah Ma's picture inside and placed it next to her husband's on the family altar of ancestor worship. Da Wei and his mother followed him inside. Da Wei laid the orchid next to her picture.

"I think she is here with us." said Da Wei.

"Of course, she is," said his father. "Just like we are here for each other." Da Wei's mother put her arm around him.

They stood silently for a few moments in the circle of love. Then his parents went quietly into the courtyard.

Da Wei left the cool, dark room and wandered outside into the sunlight where his friends were playing tag. An unexpected lightness came over him as he watched Li Zhi run from one person to the next. Da Wei moved closer. The heaviness of the past several days melted away as the game enveloped him. His hands clapped when Li Zhi tagged his classmate, Mao Sheng.

"You're it!" she cried.

"No I'm not!" yelled Mao Sheng, as he lunged for Da Wei. Da Wei dodged Mao Sheng's touch and ran into the street to join his friends.

Returning to
the Ancestral Home

◆

Mao Sheng and his father, the elementary school teacher, Mr. Wang, surveyed the vast checkerboard of cultivated land from the train window. Several farmers wearing bamboo hats were bent over the flooded rice fields.

"Do you remember our trip here two years ago?" His father pointed to the small, tractorlike machine chugging through the mud. "Then there were more water buffalo plowing the fields."

Mao Sheng mumbled, "Sort of." He didn't want to answer. He'd much rather be back at home warming up with his teammates for the soccer game. They needed him. After all, he was the center forward, and today was the big playoff against Dong Shan Middle School.

"Why did I have to come?" asked Mao Sheng. "Ma Ma and Shou Mei stayed at home."

"You are Lao Da, the eldest brother," said his father. "It's an honor to come back to the ancestral home, where your grandfather was born and I was born and you were born. Besides," he continued, "we need to stay with grandfather while uncle and his family are away."

Mao Sheng looked out the window at the sugarcane leaning away from the passing train. He checked his watch. The game was about to start. In his mind's eye the referee blew the whistle and his friend Da Wei rushed for the ball after the starting kick. It should have been Mao Sheng rushing for the ball!

He sighed heavily and dozed off for a while, dreaming that he was back at school playing soccer. Unconsciously, he jumped in his sleep.

"Are you okay?" asked his father.

Half awake, Mao Sheng looked out on the rice fields and saw a miniature pagoda that housed the statue of a local harvest god.

"See those brick factories?" his father pointed. "They weren't here two years ago." He continued, almost to himself, "There are so many more buildings now."

Mao Sheng noticed that the houses were getting closer together and there were banana trees in some of the yards.

"We're almost there," said his father.

The train slowed and Mao Sheng now saw bunches of bananas clinging, like sleeping monkeys, to the heavy, tattered trees.

"The town's so small," said Mao Sheng. "There's hardly anything here."

The whistle sounded as the train pulled into the station. Mao Sheng and his father stood up and pulled their bags from the luggage holder above them. The train stopped abruptly and Mr. Wang fell backward. Mao Sheng raised his arm and blocked the fall.

"You've really gotten strong!" said his father, after recovering his balance. "It must be all that exercise from playing soccer."

Mao Sheng's face clouded. He loved helping his father, but he didn't like being reminded that he was missing the biggest soccer game of the year.

They left the station and began walking through town.

"There's only one real street?" asked Mao Sheng, looking down the narrow alleys on each side.

"Until a few years ago the main street was as narrow as the side streets. But its been widened for the traffic. When I was growing up the only transportation was water buffalo and bicycle rickshas."

Mao Sheng surveyed the street vendors and began examining some videos lined up on a makeshift table.

"Grandfather lives way out in the countryside," said his father, checking his watch. "We should get there before it's dark."

Mao Sheng's father hailed a taxi and bargained with the driver until he was satisfied with the fare. Soon they were headed for the countryside.

From the back seat Mao Sheng saw the digital clock on the dashboard. By now the game was over. He was dying to know if they'd won. If only his grandfather had a phone! Then he could call one of his teammates and find out the score.

"I'm glad we moved to Chiai," said Mao Sheng.

"I am, too," said his father. "But I still love coming back to the countryside."

Mao Sheng shifted in his seat. They had been traveling a long time and he was sleepy. Rousing himself, he looked out at the bright orange sunset above the rice fields. A lone scarecrow, topped with a bamboo hat, guarded the harvest.

"Aren't we going backward?" asked Mao Sheng.

"You're right," said his father. "We passed by here on the train. It won't be long now. It's just up on the left."

The sky was darkening quickly and Mao Sheng's eyes strained to see what was ahead.

"There it is!" exclaimed his father, pointing to a lighted farmhouse surrounded by a flooded rice field.

His father paid the driver, and the taxi drove away. For a moment they stood in the quiet, staring out at the crude, mud-brick dwelling overflowing with light.

"Let's go," said his father, heading for the nearest levy. Mao Sheng picked up his bag and jacket and followed his father along the middle of the narrow ridge, careful not to slip into the flooded field. Step by step, the glowing light increased in size until they stood beside it. His father pushed open the door.

"Ah Ba, Ah Ba," he said, hurrying over to a thin old man seated at a round wooden table. The old man pushed his chair back. "Don't get up," said Mao Sheng's father, putting his hand on Ah Ba's arm. Mao Sheng and his father sat down at the table, across from the oil lamp.

Mao Sheng thought Ah Ba seemed much older than he remembered him. He looked into the warm, brown eyes that glowed from the lamp's light and listened as his grandfather told them how he'd been ill, but now was feeling much better.

"Da Ge's wife fixed food before they left." Ah Ba pointed to a small cupboard. "Please, help yourself."

Mao Sheng and his father set the table with rice bowls and chopsticks and then put out the dishes of duck, dried meat, rice and asparagus.

While eating, Mao Sheng listened to Ah Ba talk about the exceptionally good rice harvest they'd had. "We're planning to buy two more acres with our savings and the extra money from this crop." Then he turned to Mao Sheng.

"How are your grades this year?"

"He's number two in his class," said Mao Sheng's father, proudly. "And, he's the starting center forward for the school's champion soccer team."

Mao Sheng cringed when his father's arm went around him. He was still angry about missing the game.

Ah Ba's weathered face shone, as if surrounded by a halo, through the lantern's failing light. "What a wonderful grandson you are! We are so fortunate to have you in the family."

Mao Sheng blushed. He remembered how he'd resisted visiting his grandfather.

"The lamp's very low," said Mao Sheng's father. "We should be getting ready for bed."

"You know where everything is," said Ah Ba, going slowly over to the altar of ancestor worship. He struck a match and lit a stick of incense. Mao Sheng and his father came over and stood next to him. All of them put their hands together and prayed while bowing slightly to the altar.

Ah Ba finished and looked over at Mao Sheng. "They're helping take care of us," he said.

Mao Sheng remembered the missed soccer game and thought: why didn't the gods intercede so that I could come to grandfather's next weekend instead?

"I'll sleep down here where I usually do," said Grandfather, pointing to the small bed in the corner. "You two can sleep upstairs."

Mao Sheng and his father got ready for bed and then went up the ladder to the loft. Almost as soon as Mao Sheng's head touched the mattress, he fell asleep.

All of a sudden, he woke to the sound of his name being called.

"Mao Sheng! Wake up! Hurry!" yelled his father. "Ah Ba is hurt!"

Mao Sheng sat up in the dark and looked over the edge of the loft. "Hurry up!" yelled his father.

He quickly slid down the ladder and came over to his father. Fearfully, he looked into his grandfather's ashen face.

"He fell trying to get a drink of water, and I think his leg is broken. We'll have to take him to a doctor. Run out to the road. Flag down the first car and show him how to come down the driveway. Take the lantern over there. It has more oil. Hurry up!"

Mao Sheng lit the lantern, put on his shoes and ran out the door. He ran frantically up the muddy driveway while praying for a car to come into view.

Mao Sheng was still tense and frightened when two bright headlights finally appeared. He swung the lantern wildly until the car pulled over to the side.

"Hurry! Come help my grandfather!" yelled Mao Sheng desperately.

He ran ahead of the car, guiding it with the lantern, until they reached the farmhouse. The man jumped from the car and ran into the house with him. He spent a few moments checking Ah Ba over and then asked Mao Sheng to bring him two pieces of firewood. "We'll need some cord or wide tape," he said. Mao Sheng found some twine in the cabinet.

The man carefully slipped the wider piece of firewood under Ah Ba's injured leg and put the other one on top of it. "I learned how to do this in the army," he said, circling the leg with twine. "He'll be all right. We'll take him to the hospital so a doctor can set the leg and check him over."

"We can't thank you enough," said Mao Sheng's father.

"I'm glad he stopped me," said the young man, glancing at Mao Sheng. "You're quite a lantern-waver. If you hadn't been waving it so energetically I never would have stopped."

Flooded with pride, Mao Sheng smiled shyly. It was the same feeling he had, only much more wonderful, when people praised him for winning a soccer game. He thought about his family and how he loved belonging to it—even more than belonging to his soccer team. Then he looked down at his grandfather and realized, for the first time, that he was in the right place this weekend after all.

Ping Mei's Wish

◆

Ping Mei walked home from school the long way so she could stop at the market and buy a bean cake. It was her favorite treat but her mother didn't buy them often because they were so expensive.

"Which one will it be?" asked Mr. Feng as she breathed on his glass case.

Ping Mei looked back and forth at the mung and black bean cakes. "Lu dou bing," she said, pointing to the mung bean cake. Mr. Feng reached in and picked up a round, flaky pastry. Ping Mei took the cake and paid him 30 yuan. Before taking a bite, she mouthed the red Chinese characters stamped on the top.

She visualized writing the characters in their correct stroke order and then thought of the grade she'd gotten today in Chinese on her report card. Ninety-three. Ninety-three, she said again to herself. Two points short of ninety-five which was what she needed to go to Ali Shan.

She thought of the picture of Yu Shan, Jade Mountain, above her bed, torn from last year's calendar. It was ringed in a sea of clouds infused with pink light. Yu Shan at sunrise. It had been her dream to rise before dawn at Ali Shan and view this spectacular sight.

Ping Mei sighed deeply, wrapped the rest of her bean cake in paper and stuck it inside her backpack. She looked up and saw Li Zhi coming toward her.

"Ni hao?" she greeted Ping Mei. "How did you do on your report card?"

Ping Mei hung her head. "All right, but not good enough."

"What do you mean?" asked Li Zhi, sucking on a stalk of sugarcane.

"Last report period my father said if I brought all my grades up to ninety-five he would take me to Ali Shan on the train."

"Let's see," said Li Zhi.

Ping Mei reached into her backpack and pulled out a slip of paper.

Li Zhi examined it closely. "Ninety-three in Chinese."

"I know," said Ping Mei sadly.

"Why don't you change it?"

"What?"

"Change it."

"How?"

"Look," said Li Zhi, tracing the ninety-three intently with her fingernail, "Just take a pen and continue the curve on the top and bottom of the three. Then it says ninety-eight."

"That's cheating!" exclaimed Ping Mei. "I could never do that. Besides," she said thoughtfully, "Mr. Wang would notice when I brought it back."

"No he won't. He doesn't even check the grades again. I know because Jia Shing did it. He changed a seventy-two to a ninety-two by making a circle on the top of the seven."

"Jia Shing!" said Ping Mei, in disbelief.

"I know," said Li Zhi. "I couldn't believe it either. But Zong Zong told me she saw him do it."

"I'd be afraid to do it."

"It's up to you," said Li Zhi. "But if I was dying to go to Ali Shan, I would." She bit into the soft, white center of the sugarcane. "I have to babysit Mei Mei while my mother goes shopping. See you tomorrow." She disappeared into the crowd.

Ping Mei took the half-finished bean cake from her backpack. But this time she chewed on the sweet filling without tasting it. Changing her grade wouldn't hurt anyone. Unless someone discovered what she'd done. She shuddered, thinking about it. The worst thing would be if her parents found out. But if Jia Shing had gotten away with it, she probably could, too.

She imagined the hotel at Ali Shan. It would be the first time, ever, she had slept in one. During the day they would visit the pagoda on the edge of the Two Sister's Pond. Her mother had told her many times how the pagoda's image was reflected perfectly in the water and how she and Ping Mei's father had visited it shortly after they were married.

Ping Mei passed through the produce stalls and noticed the neatly stacked rows of eggplant. She picked one up and looked closely at the shiny dark surface.

"Can I help you?" asked the vendor, smiling.

"Oh, no," said Ping Mei, putting the eggplant back exactly where she had found it. She moved quickly to the next stall which was filled with mangos. Her mouth watered at the sight of them. If only she hadn't spent all her money on the sweet bean cake. She hoped her mother had something delicious today for an after-school treat.

Maybe her father would give her another chance. If all her grades were at least ninety-five next report period he might still take her to Ali Shan. But that was so far away.

Hurriedly she moved through the fish market, fearful of seeing the live fish whisked from a bucket of water and disemboweled before her. The gruesome image of their death made her shiver.

A horrible thought crossed her mind. What if she died before the end of the next report period? She had a cousin in Taipei, her father's sister's son, who seemed fine and then one morning he didn't wake up. Ping Mei's eyes welled with tears. What if she never got a chance to see Ali Shan!

She reached her apartment building and stopped. Li Zhi's advice, "If I were you and was dying to go to Ali Shan, I'd do it," echoed in her mind.

This was the last chance to change her Chinese grade. It would be so easy just to take her pen—it was exactly the same color as Mr. Wang's—and make two small, almost indistinguishable curves that seemed very harmless, but to her would make all the difference in the world. Ping Mei looked down at her backpack. She knew exactly where the pen was.

The three-generation tree at Ali Shan came to mind. Although she had never seen it, she imagined one huge tree growing out of another and then another tree growing out of that one. Ping Mei thought not only of how disappointed her parents would be if they knew she had altered her grade but also how disappointed she would be in herself. Even if no one ever found out.

She turned slowly and walked up the steps of her building. As she opened the door to her apartment, her mother turned from the sink.

"Ni hao? Did you have a good day at school?" she asked.

Ping Mei dropped her backpack and slid into a kitchen chair. "Okay, I guess," she answered.

Her mother opened the refrigerator and handed her a small carton with a straw attached to the side. "Here's one of your favorites, pineapple-coconut juice."

Ping Mei opened the carton and began drinking. She heard footsteps coming up the stairs. "Here comes Dad," she said quietly, hoping he wouldn't remember it was report card day.

He walked in the door. "How's my favorite nine-year-old?" He patted her on the shoulders and sat down.

"Oh, fine," she answered.

"And how's your report card?"

Ping Mei's heart sank. Mechanically she bent over and pulled it out of her backpack. "I really tried in Chinese," she spoke quickly. "I had a ninety-six average until the last test." She paused, on the verge of tears. "But it was so hard. That's why the grade's low."

Ping Mei's mother bent over her husband's shoulder and read the rest of the subjects.

"Ninety-eight in history, ninety-seven in science, ninety-eight in geography, ninety-nine in citizenship and ninety-eight in math. Wow! That's a great report card."

"But not good enough to go to Ali Shan," said Ping Mei sadly.

"Well, I don't know," said her father. "I bet if we averaged all these together you'd have at least a ninety-five."

Ping Mei was afraid to hope.

"And I think," said her father, "that a ninety-five average is good enough to go to Ali Shan."

Ping Mei hopped up from her chair and began jumping around the room. "I can't wait. I can't wait," she cried. "When can we go?"

"How about this weekend?" asked her father.

Ping Mei ran to the window and looked way down the narrow street to the train tracks. She imagined herself sitting in the dining car, running her hands over the smooth, white linen tablecloth. Already she was on the way to Ali Shan.

Zong Zong Goes to Disneyland

◆

Zong Zong gazed out the car window at the long row of pink and white oleander growing out of the median. She had never seen so many cars and such wide highways. Beyond them, the greenish-brown hills of southern California were dotted with houses and brightly colored flowering trees and shrubs.

"Meiguo," she said quietly.

"What?" asked her American cousin Cheryl.

"Beautiful country." She translated the Chinese words which actually meant "United States."

"It's true," said her aunt, in Chinese. "The name fits the country."

Then Cheryl said something in English that Zong Zong didn't understand. If only Cheryl would speak Chinese, thought Zong Zong. Then she wouldn't feel so left out. Her aunt and uncle were always very kind and remembered to speak in Chinese, but Cheryl chattered constantly in English. And when her mother reminded Cheryl, she'd whine and complain, "I can't remember all the words. I understand, but speaking is too hard."

Suddenly Zong Zong's stomach made a loud gurgle, and Cheryl burst out laughing. Zong Zong's face burned.

"It's probably the breakfast cereal," said her aunt. "Your stomach still hasn't adjusted to the milk."

It was true. Zong Zong felt a little sick. She never drank milk at home. Chinese people didn't have the enzyme needed to digest cow's milk, unless they drank it several times. If only her aunt would make chi fan for breakfast. She didn't even care about eating it plain, without meat and pickled vegetables. The dry crunchy cereal was so unappetizing; either it stuck to the roof of her mouth or it was too soggy.

"We're almost there," said her aunt. "Only one more exit."

Zong Zong leaned forward and looked ahead. She recalled how jealous all her friends in Mr. Wang's class were when she told them she was going to the United States and would visit Disneyland.

She looked over at the big car in the lane next to her. Rarely did she see these cars in Taiwan. Only a few people could afford them. Her family didn't even own a car. They lived in a small apartment. It was nothing like the spacious house with a large, landscaped yard that her cousin lived in.

A wave of embarrassment came over her. What if Cheryl came to Taiwan? She didn't even have her own room. Her whole family lived in three rooms. She and her sister slept on a couch in the living room, and her parents slept in the only bedroom.

"There it is!" exclaimed Cheryl, pointing off to the right.

Zong Zong looked over and saw the snowcapped Matterhorn, just as they exited the freeway.

Her aunt pulled into the huge parking lot and Zong Zong could barely contain her excitement. One of her most exciting dreams was coming true. Everyone got out and Zong Zong and Cheryl raced to the ticket window.

"Where do you want to go first?" asked her aunt, after purchasing the tickets.

"Let's go to Star Wars," said Cheryl, "before it's too crowded."

Zong Zong followed Cheryl's rapid twists and turns through the wide walkways until they reached the line of people waiting to see Star Wars.

"After this, let's go to the Haunted House," said Cheryl. Then she held up her finger and spoke to Zong Zong in broken Chinese. "But we're not going to Pirates of the Caribbean," she said, emphatically shaking her head.

"Wei shenmo?" asked Zong Zong.

"Because," began Cheryl dramatically, "we went when I was little and it scared me so much that I started crying."

"You'd probably like it now that you're older," said her mother.

"No way!"

Zong Zong looked around. Everywhere men with dustpans and brooms whisked trash out of the way. America was very clean, and this was the cleanest place she'd seen in the past four days. She wondered if it was the cleanest place in the world.

They walked through the doors to Star Wars and began going up the spiral staircase. The loudspeaker blared with interplanetary announcements and robots moved back and forth. Replicas of space stations and spaceships hung from the ceiling.

"Are those real?" she asked, pointing to a rocket ship.

Cheryl laughed and, again, Zong Zong blushed. "They're all make-believe," she said confidently. "The real ones are much bigger."

Zong Zong wished Cheryl would like her. She decided to be more careful of what she said. She hated sounding stupid.

She thought of a cousin from the countryside who had stayed at her home in Chiai. She hadn't even known how to flush the toilet. Zong Zong was sorry she hadn't been kinder to her.

The doors in front of them opened and they stepped inside the theater.

"Let's sit in the front," said Cheryl, grabbing her arm.

"Maybe the middle is better," said her aunt. "Especially if Zong Zong's stomach isn't well."

Cheryl frowned.

"I'm fine," said Zong Zong, wanting to please Cheryl.

They sat down in the front and fastened their seat belts.

"It's really scary at first," whispered Cheryl. "But don't worry. Just relax and you'll get used to it."

The screen lit up and the ride through space began. Zong Zong stayed with it until she felt her stomach turn. Then she put her hand over her mouth and squeezed her eyes shut. What if she threw up! All her wonderful dreams about the United States and Disneyland disappeared with this humiliating thought.

When the lights came on, her hand dropped from her mouth and she managed a weak smile. Her aunt looked at her askance.

"Are you all right?" she asked.

"Fine, fine," Zong Zong lied.

"Let's try something a little quieter."

"The Haunted House," cried Cheryl.

"All right," said her mother.

They exited Star Wars and Cheryl took off. Zong Zong finally caught up with her in line at the Haunted House.

"You'll really like this," said Cheryl. "It's so mysterious, and a little scary. Uh, oh!" she cried. "I have to go to the bathroom."

"It's back over there, just around the corner," Cheryl's mother said.

"Come with me," said Cheryl.

"But what about Zong Zong?" asked her mother.

"She can save our places. Look how long the line is. We don't want to start all over again."

"Do you mind?" asked her aunt.

"Oh, no," said Zong Zong, trying not to sound worried.

"Just follow the line," said her aunt. "If we don't get back in time, go in and take the ride. We'll meet you outside in five or ten minutes, when we've finished. Okay?"

"Okay," said Zong Zong, nodding her head. But inside she was afraid.

She watched them disappear and then turned back around. In a few minutes the group in front of her went through the door. Next it would be her turn.

Zong Zong kept turning around, hoping to see Cheryl and her mother. She thought of Kuan Yin, the small green ceramic goddess on the bookshelf at home. The door opened and fearfully she began praying silently to the goddess. The surrounding crowd carried her through the open door and into the elevator.

After exiting the elevator she followed the crowd and stepped into a "Doom Buggy." At first she enjoyed the ride and was fascinated with the eerie Victorian rooms. Then a strange, floating, gossamerlike object caught her eye. The buggy brought her closer and she realized it was a man's head, perfectly shaped with a vivid and lively face.

She stiffened in fright. Of course she knew spirits existed. But in Taiwan they weren't visible. Some people had claimed to see them, but she never had. Nor did she want to. She looked ahead. There were several more spirits: women and children. She wanted to scream: "Let me out of here!" Is this how they made money in America? By imprisoning spirits so they couldn't go to the afterworld?

Zong Zong stared into their faces. They looked so *real*. She grabbed hold of the buggy. Surely, she would be punished for participating in this awful show.

Quickly she prayed to Kuan Yin. "Please, please forgive me for not being able to set these spirits free. And please, please help me to get out of here safely. And bless my family. Bring me back to them soon."

The buggy turned quickly. She faced a mirror and saw a ghost next to her. Zong Zong opened her mouth to scream but nothing came out. Frantically she jumped from the buggy and stepped onto the moving sidewalk. Suddenly the door opened and Zong Zong ran outside to a nearby bench and collapsed. She put her head in her hands and continued praying fervently—this time for Cheryl and her aunt. What if the spirits revolted while they were in there and the building collapsed?

"Zong Zong, Zong Zong." She heard her name and felt a hand on her shoulder. She looked up and saw her aunt. Then she burst into tears.

"Why are the spirits there?" she cried.

"They're not spirits," said her aunt, putting her arm around her. "It's just a trick. It's not real."

"Are you sure?" asked Zong Zong, wiping her eyes.

"I felt the same way when I saw Pirates of the Caribbean," said Cheryl. "I was so scared!" She gave Zong Zong a hug.

For the first time in America, she felt a part of things.

"I know," said Cheryl, pulling Zong Zong up from the bench. "Let's go on the teacup ride. "Believe me," she said confidently, "that will be fun."

Hand in hand, they ran off toward Fantasyland.

About Each Story

---◆---

The Abacus Contest

The abacus is used to add, subtract, multiply, divide and calculate square and cubic roots. Children as young as four or five years old may begin taking abacus lessons. Different levels of expertise on the abacus are determined by championship competitions. Until the advent of the calculator, the abacus was utilized throughout the Chinese world in shops and banks for business and commerce. It is still used in Chinese schools and is a valuable tool for teaching arithmetic.

Bright Eyes

Pigeon racing originated with the ancient Egyptians and Persians three thousand years ago and then spread to other parts of the world. It is common for people to raise homing pigeons in Taiwan and race them. The money collected by registering pigeons for each race is then distributed as prize money to the winners. Compared with people's salaries, the prize money is considerable, so very good care is taken of racing pigeons.

Saying Good-bye to Ah Ma

Customarily, a newly married couple comes to live at the husband's family home. Most people farm or are in business, and many people are needed to help earn the family living. Often several families live in the same house. Thus children may grow up not only with their parents and grandparents but also with their aunts, uncles and cousins.

Returning to the Ancestral Home

Some of the religious beliefs in Taiwan and China are based on Confucian philosophy. This dictates that people should have a great deal of care and respect for the social order and family members. Thus it's very important to honor and care for one's parents. Ancestors, worshipped at the family altar, are held in reverence because, as spirits, they have access to the gods and may intercede and answer the prayers of those still on earth.

Ping Mei's Wish

Education has, for many centuries, been an important part of Chinese culture. As far back as 2200 B.C. merit exams were given to those who wished to enter government service. Stories abound in Chinese litera-ture and folklore about poor peasants who became prominent and well-to-do overnight after making the highest grade on a government merit exam.

Zong Zong Goes to Disneyland

The people in Taiwan and China pray to many different gods. Religion is a combination of Bud-dhism, the worship of various local gods and doing good works; Confucianism, ancestor worship and adherence to high ethical standards; and Taoism, the admonition to live a simple, contemplative life in harmony with the universe. Many people in Taiwan and China are very conscious of the spirit world and believe it influences their day-to-day lives.

Glossary

$\blacklozenge$

Ali Shan: The town in Taiwan where the highest mountain in this part of the world, Yu Shan, is located. At more than 13,000 feet, it is higher than Mt. Fuji in Japan.

Bao Zhi (bow zher): Large, thick, doughy dumplings filled with meat, vegetables or sweet bean paste. It is originally a northern Chinese dish.

Bicycle Ricksha: A light, two-wheeled cart once widely used as a public vehicle in Asian cities. The original rickshas were powered by a runner who ran between the shafts. Later models placed a bicycle or a motorcycle between the shafts to power the cart. Although still popular in some smaller Asian cities, they have been banned in most large ones because authorities feel using humans for pulling heavy loads is undignified.

Chi Fan (chee-fan): A rice porridge with a soft, mushy consistency. It is the daily breakfast diet in most Asian countries, and in Taiwan it is often eaten with plain or pickled vegetables, meat or fish.

Chiai (chee ah yi): A medium-sized city in southern Taiwan with a population of approximately 500,000 people.

Chiang Kai-shek: The leader of the Koumindeng or Nationalist party who fled mainland China, after being defeated by Communist forces, and established a government in Taiwan. He took full military and civil control of Taiwan in 1949 after supressing the Taiwanese independence movement. He remained in power until his death in 1975.

Da Ge: Older brother. Confucian titles denoting respect for elders and those of a higher rank or station begin in the home. All older brothers are known as Da Ge. By the same token, all younger brothers are known as De De.

Harvest God: Often in Taiwan, especially on country roadsides, there are small shrines for local gods. These gods are the administrators of the area and are prayed to by the local inhabitants for their basic needs, including a good harvest.

Kaohsiung (cow shung): Taiwan's second-largest city after the capital, Taipei. A busy seaport, it is located on the southwest coast of Taiwan.

Kuan Yin: The name of a very popular Buddhist goddess worshippped in Southeast Asia. She is a goddess of compassion.

Lao Da: Interchangeable with Da Ge, oldest brother, and is also used between men to denote respect for another man who is older.

Jian Zhi (jeean-zher): A game, similar to hacky-sack, played by school-children in Taiwan and China. A small, weighted leather disk with feathers, called a jian zhi, is kept in the air by kicking it. The winner is the one who can kick the jian zhi the greatest number of times before it hits the ground.

Lu Dou Bing: Mandarin Chinese for green bean cake. A flaky, round cake usually about two inches across filled with sweetened mung bean paste. Similar cakes may also be filled with black bean paste or other sweets.

Mainland China: The People's Republic of China on the Asian continent. It should not be confused with the Republic of China on the island of Taiwan. It is approximately the size of the United States and, with 1.2 billion people, has approximately one-fifth of the world's population.

Mandarin: The Chinese dialect that originated in northern China and Beijing. The Chinese call the dialect *putonghua*, which means "common language." Today it is the official language of both the People's Republic of China (mainland China) and the Republic of China (Taiwan).

Mei Mei (may may): Younger sister.

Ni hao (nee how): A Mandarin Chinese greeting that means "hello," or a familiar "how are you?"

Pagoda: A type of tower, commonly associated with Buddhist temples, which sometimes contains shrines or images. It usually has from three to fifteen stories of decreasing size from bottom to top. Each story has a roof that curves upward on the edges, supposedly to deflect evil spirits that fall toward the earth. Chinese people believe a pagoda brings wealth and happiness to the surrounding community.

Taipei: The capital and largest city in Taiwan. It has a population of over two million people, and the name means "northern Taiwan." The Chinese founded Taipei in 1708.

Taitung: A city on the southeast coast of Taiwan.

Taiwan: A mountainous island in the South China Sea about ninety miles off the coast of the People's Republic of China. The name means "terraced bay" in Mandarin. Portuguese explorers named it Ilha Formosa, which means "beautiful island." It is 235 miles long and 90 miles wide and has approximately twenty million people.

Year of the Cow: Chinese astrology has twelve animals on the zodiac. The cow is one of them. Relationships between the animals are determined by the distances between them in the circle. Some of the relationships are considered positive, good omens, while others are considered negative. The distance between the cow and the rat on the Chinese zodiac is considered a negative aspect, and thus, it is bad luck for a person born in the year of the rat to witness the burial of one born in the year of the cow.

Yuan: The monetary denomination of currency in Taiwan. Currently, twenty-six yuan equals one U.S. dollar.

Wei Shenmo (way shenmo): The Mandarin words for "why."